Beyond the Road

Matrika Press is proud to publish
this book of poetry
by JT Curran.

Beyond the Road

JT Curran

Matrika Press
Publisher

Copyright © JT Curran

July 2017

All Rights Reserved
including the right of reproduction,
copying, or storage in any form
or means, including electronic,
In Whole or Part,
without prior written
permission of the author

ISBN: 978-1-946088-01-7

Library of Congress Control Number: 2017907754
1.Poetry 2.Title

Matrika Press
164 Lancey Street
Pittsfield, Maine
(760) 889-5428
Editor@MatrikaPress.com

Matrika Press

www.MatrikaPress.com

Arranged by: Jason Curran
Cover Design by: Aaron Curran
Photography by: Kate Peters
Interior Design by: "Twinkle" Marie Manning
Cover Painting: Bob Loughrey
Interior Art by: JT Curran

Printed in the USA

"Listen
      I am getting ready
          to say
              something
          Very
                  Poignant"

- JT Curran

Author's Dedication

To Diane,
My Personal Muse.

Beyond the Road

JT Curran

TABLE OF CONTENTS

Foreword - 18

I - Early Stuff - 21
    Bobby, My Man
    RFK
    Hey man it's Saturday
    Oh recreant night
    The late light
    The leaves of summer
    When the Ferris Wheel
    God?
    Haiku
    She slipped gently 'cross the snow

II - Love & War - 33
    Cape May 1969
    A Korean fly
    9 DEC 69
    December 13, 1969
    Gilded gold edged clouds
    I saw you rise
    Watch
    Wait

III - Confessions of a Twice Removed Dirt Farmer - 47
    Mexico
    Paradise Destroyed
    What a day!
    Hey lil bird
    Justify It Oh lord
    On Sleep

IV - Psychological Psandwiches - 57

    Beverly
    Bones
    Charlie Stearns
    Dr. Shrink
    Harold
    Leighton Sewer
    Peter Calliope
    Sam S.
    The devil came to Carl
    The Secretary of Perjury

V - Observations & Obstacles - 75

    Hey Johnny boy
    Snow bound
    Exit
    A little ripple
    With trembling heart
    Gabriel
    Mr. Jones
    Disaster
    Yo Brian
    Reminiscing again
    Ackley
    Kentucky Derby
    Watergate
    Running
    The king of bebop passed away
    Just keeps getting

VI - Depression City Whew!
1977 in Review - 97

    Hey Clay
    Quebec City
    Depression Seventy Seven

Oh the things you could've done
What's going on?
A very good gesture
One Two Three
His words were
Words
The verge

VII - Flying Without Wings - 109

Oh those eyes
Big tits
Budding little girl
She smiles
I sense the fear
Terrorist
History in the making
Before Kids
Winter snows and
Sweeping snows
Butterball
I saw you standing by the
I drove across that bridge
Raise the flags
No privacy!
The years pass by
My world
Walking down the path
Alone
Iron Ann
Cold
It's just a phase
Sometimes

VIII - Reflections & Interjections - 135

I woke up in a different world
Paste his picture on
Florida - April 2007
The turkeys are horny
The scales
That smirky little smile
Something
Watch the money
It's me
Paris
Erectile dysfunction
You bitch
The
There ain't nuthin'
The hills are alive
Been there
Are you living in fear
The garden
There ain't
The big bang
I felt
Woke up this morning
You
Sign me up!
At least
Gathering shit
The hearse
The nice things
Time was
Crazy!
Memorial Day
Emily
Assisted living
Helicopter time

IX - Mostly 9 - 171

    Whenever I hear
    Danny Boy
    The Sunday crowd
    Coming back
    Remember
    P.J.
    She
    My hero
    Compromise
    Sitting
    Sagging
    Make your
    Dr. Chuck
    Collateral
    He likely
    Sanderlings
    The streetlight
    I
    The father
    The bar
    The problem
    All that
    Perspectives
    The apple fell
    The sun
    Whispering
    Mostly money she said

X - Hodgepodge, Olio and Other Scraps - 201

    Buffalo
    Ya ever notice
    Sun shining
    Stalking round the room
    Expensive suits

My whiteness
Another hero
We watched……..
The boxes lined
I thought I was teaching you
Used to be
Don't know much
I remember
Somewhat like Caesar
To Donald
Too bad you're

XI - Splitting Wood and Other Mindless Tasks - 219

Chomped
Ripples
Lined up
Ya
Doing
Sheer White
The hills
Driving around
(Cuatro de Mayo)
Indiscretions
Won't be long
Gospel
Parables
Breaking up
Just wondering
Ran
The swamp
Time to
Reality
Daze
They're

  Dressed in camo
  Have you noticed
  Weather
  Snow
  Facebook
  Take a walk
  2 days ago
  Hell
  Left wing
  Bones
  She paced
  Cyberspace
  4 Coronas
  The band
  Simply
  Dennis Hopper
  Seems

XII - The Red Book -
Between the Holidays - 263

  The sexes
  Another
  Dark
  ?
  Loon
  Independence
  The sun
  I wish
  August 6 or 7
  Man
  9-11 eve
  The shadows
  The Hippies
  Honking
  I was
  It

Beyond the Road

November
Just when
The remote
Here son
Muffled applause
As
Diminished
Anticipation
The stars
Perplexing
Eating
Been
The guys
We

XIII - Recent Work - 297

Summer Solstice
Clare
Jack
Burt
Hey kid
All
Put the boy
Mill towns
All Saints
Sometimes
What
We'd
Gathered
Legacy
Roller skating
Breezy
Need
Birthday eve
I've been thinking
Trying

JT Curran

That 54 Cadillac
The late night train
The silence
Concussion
Wish

Special Thanks - 324

Publisher's Note - 326

About the Author - 327

Foreword

This book of poems is something that I've wanted to do for many years and have put it off probably due to fear of putting myself on the firing line. But thanks to my thoughtful and loving children, I am now in the position to make a dream come true. And as I sift through fifty years of poetry I find the task a bit daunting.
In fact it scares the hell out of me as I wonder what pieces to put down on paper.
I write in diary sized notebooks. When the pages are filled I title the book and move on to a new one. I was just going to publish one of the books but after consideration, I felt that I should make it selected poems - some stuff from all the books over the years. Reading some of my early poetry is somewhat painful as I see how young and naive I was. Fifty years of poetry is a lot of ups and downs and a lot of growth - the good, the bad and the ugly.
    I entered high school in 1959, an all boys Catholic high school where learning was secondary to be being cool. I had an English teacher who was new and had a passion for poetry that came through when he tried to teach us. If I had admitted to my classmates and friends that I was interested, I would have

been ostracized and made to feel like an outcast. So secretly I read the poems at home. Gerard Manley Hopkins was the first one who opened up my eyes as I read his works and eventually began to see his sprung rhythm as Mr. McBride had told the class.

The beatnik era crept onto the scene and I found myself going to a couple of coffee shops where there was poetry readings, folk music, chess, lots of bearded young men and espresso. I loved it but it still wasn't cool at school. So, I put poetry on the back burner, graduated from high school, worked for a couple of years and then headed off to college and by Junior or Senior year began to write. I discovered Lawrence Ferlinghetti, e e cummings, T. S. Eliot, Rimbaud, the beat poets - on and on. I liked the shortness of Emily Dickinson, the characters of Edwin Arlington Robinson and the free range of the beats.

Like most poets, I write when I hear a word or phrase or have a feeling. It comes from somewhere else and winds up on the page. I have tried to include a wide range of poems from the late 60's to the present. I find some of my early work a bit embarrassing but hopefully the reader will see the passion and growth and find this stimulating and meaningful or at least entertaining.

Beyond the Road

JT Curran

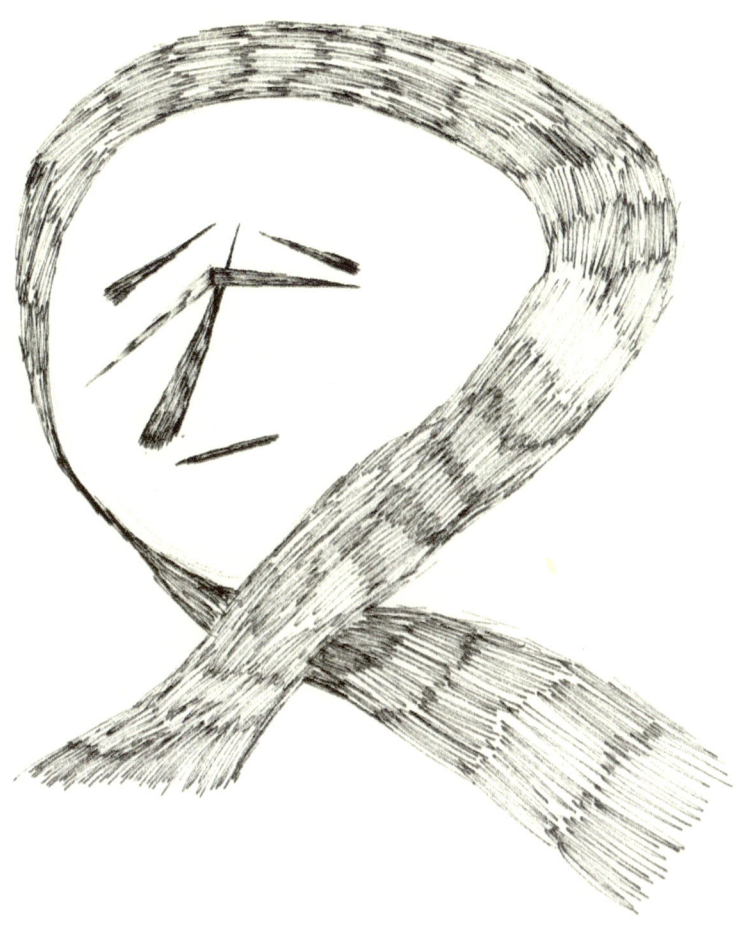

I - EARLY STUFF

Bobby, My Man
Remember Texas
The summer of 1965
    You, me and that white convertible
Top down
Screaming across that Oklahoma night
    Beer cans flying
    Young hearts sighing
Waiting for Mexico
Racing to Mexico
    And all those señoritas
    your brother told us about

RFK

"Mine eyes have seen the glory......."
    great men and small men
    white men and black men
    rich men and poor men
    good men and bad men
    ALL MEN
Sang the song
    with tear filled eyes
And for one moment
    they were united
Violence had ceased
while the hearse carried RFK
    to his final resting place
His loss
    felt throughout the nation
    gained what he so much desired
    for a few short hours of history
But after his lowering into the ground
    the hate returns
    the peace is lost
    men turn against men
        and his death was all in vain
        the mourning after

Beyond the Road

Hey man it's Saturday
    Time to hit the stool
You buy I'll fly cause it's
    Time to play the fool

        Put the ten spot on the bar
        See how fast it goes
        Warm your cells numb your tongue
        Just a habit I suppose

Brothers
Every Sadday without fail
Might as well be prisoners
    might as well be jail

Drink up Drink up
While you're shaking inside
Drink up Drink up
All the things that you tried

        Hear all your brain cells go
        clickety clack
        Wondering why your world's
        out of whack
        Wondering
            just what the fuck
            is happening

JT Curran

Oh recreant night
    satan's son
    unleashing
        the enemies of my saneness
        to wage war upon the battlefield
            my mind

Who sucks the
    warmth and friendliness
    from the sky
        leaving the land desolate
        destroying all in sight

The barrens of the underworld
    devour the horizon
    increasing in numbers
        like vultures swooping down
        on death's decay

Seeping through my door
    creeping crawling
    suddenly surrounding
        holding me captive
        'til dawn's delight

Beyond the Road

The late light
        burns
Through the trees
        the earth turns
Walking waves
        break
On the beach
        I lie awake
    Not alone
        Soft long hair
            envelopes my face
        Locked together
            a warm embrace
        Flesh glistening
            moist from the moon
        Love lost and found
            too short too soon
A seagull shrieks
        in the morning sun
We wash in the water
        our work is done
Our offering to
        the goddess of night
She walks along the sands
        and slowly
            fades
              out
                  of sight

JT Curran

The leaves of summer
    Gone away
Unfolding dreams of
    Other days
                chilled air
                windy hair
                football games
                Autumn pains

        A young man growing
                feeling something sad
        In the grayness knowing
                all the things he had

family friends
books of zens
baseball glove
girls to love
        Nothing gone but
                deep inside
        The feelings that
                he tried to hide
        Misty eyes
                release the tears
        And down his cheeks
                fall the years

Beyond the Road

When the Ferris W
           h
              e
                 e
                    l
  STOPS
        my heart
  B-e-a-t-s
        for unknown depths
        from swaying seats
High above the skyline
    the eerie thrill
    of
        fall
            ing
      grinding gears
and racing fears
        pulling up the earth
        to catch my........
                SPLAT

JT Curran

God?
What if God
        were not
And life was just that
        Life!
Nothing after
        just eternal atoms
Floating through space
        looking
Looking for a bond
        to tell
What my few years
        upon Earth
Have seen and felt
        and heard
But who will listen
        to my glories
When after I'm gone
        I'm not

Haiku

Beauty is only snow deep
But when the snow melts
What do we call Spring

JT Curran

She slipped gently 'cross the snow
    with a baby in her arms
And a child to walk beside her
    full of love to keep them warm

While the sky above them melted
    to a waxy rosy sound
you could hear the colors singing
    as they danced upon the ground

They built a snowman in the middle
    of a drifted snowflake sea
The branches bowed around them
    in regal symmetry

They threw snowballs at each other
    and laughed in pure delight
While time stood still an instant
    and blended into white

With clothing soaking wet
    and cold they went inside
by the roaring kitchen stove
    and the peace they felt inside

Beyond the Road

JT Curran

II - LOVE & WAR

Cape May 1969

We sat upon the rocks
     as waves
          formed slowly
             crested
       then
    thundered
into the wall
the white foam
stood against
         the darkness
and the not quite full
      moon
showered the clouds
     with a warm
       glow
while the ocean's
      voice was heard
      below
We talked about things
    important things
    and I held you close
We watched
    and we were free
       with the sea

JT Curran

A Korean fly
      landed on my knee
Scram says I
      but I guess he
      didn't understand
      American
Strange!
Strange indeed!
      but
      .
      .
      .
      I said shoo
        and
      he flew............

9 DEC 69
  FTA
"9 more days"

Each morning
    (or the time we are woken up)
I stand
    through window
        looking
The panes like bars
    keep me locked
        within my mind
    My mind?
What mind son?
We are your mind
    Rows of barracks
    Rows of everything
        Dress to the right
        Dress to the right
They're pissed god didn't
        dress his trees to the
        right
Right?
Planes fly over.....
        Paratroopers
50,000 men
    all alone
   one body
   one mind
        Move out boy!

Color me green
Preoccupied with
        FREEDOM
Remember how it was to
        Walk along the beach
           To drink wine in a field
           To drive somewhere
           Wake up in the morning
                with you beside me
           To pick flowers
           To laugh
Yes! Yes!
Remember how it was to
        Live?
Death all around in the
        form of tin soldiers
           tin minds
Welcome to quick kill
        Men I'm Sgt......
What's the spirit of bayonet
        To KILL!
        To KILL!
What's the spirit of hand to hand
        To KILL
        To KILL
Let me! I'm ready!
I'll crush that dirty
motherfucker's head in
        Who?
That dirty........

Beyond the Road

Good morning Men I'm
Sgt.....and I'd like
to welcome you to hand
grenade
        BOOM
Gazing
    from my vantage point
I long
    to walk
    through the door
Never to return
Never to hear those cursed
    words
        "Fall In"
  To be able to walk
    slowly in a crooked line
My insides
    are tortured
    Such pain
My soul screams in
    Agony
  Oh God! Let me be!
But
    the day passes
    SLOWLY
And love
    must wait some more

December 13, 1969

Love like flower
Moistened by the
               Spring shower
Glistens
Listens
Waiting for the hour
      When
   opening before the
              dawning sun
   unfolds its charms
             for everyone
Few grasp
Few last
Beauty does not run
   but stands and reaches
   trying to teach us
The way
To say
You
I love

Beyond the Road

Gilded gold edged clouds
    Soft orange
    and tender gray
Slowly pushed
    the dark away
The sun began
    to warm the earth
I could not share
    the joy
        the mirth
I'm an eternal
    mile apart
From my love
From my heart
HERE
    I stand
        in formation
Great defender
    of the nation
For my country
    a life to give
Bullshit
    I want to love
    I want to live
As long as I'm
    dressed in green
I cannot keep
    my being clean
Let me go!
    Let me be!

JT Curran

Unchain my arms
      and
         set me free
To laugh
       and sing
           and run around
With Diane
    and the
        love we found

Beyond the Road

I saw you rise
with open eyes
    Stretching slumber
    From the warmth of your dreams
Lying
    on the flowered sheet
with a bewildered smile
you reached my heart
    and pulled me close
    to sink your breasts
        within my chest
You kissed me warm
        moist
        long
with lips that
    said I love you
The need was want
And wanting each other
We came together
    the juice of love
    dripping on our needs
of love
    We loved
And spent the dawning
    on the rise

JT Curran

Watch
    as days fade away
Wait
    for the slowly passing day
To end
And then
    we're one day nearer

Wait
>	For passing time
>	For moving mountains
>>	'Til
The aroma
of you
Fills my nostrils
Fills my mind
>	And fondles my heart
>>	For
>>	Ever

JT Curran

Beyond the Road

JT Curran

III - CONFESSIONS OF A TWICE REMOVED DIRT FARMER

Mexico

Mamacita Mamacita
    La fiesta es....
The brown skinned children swam in the
murky Rio Grande
Rio Grande?
    nothing grand
    like a stream formed from draining
sewers
La Señoritas, where are they?
    Ah Señor, I take you to Papgayos
    "Rubbers! Spanish Fly! French
Ticklers!
    Like a hot dog vendor at Yankee
Stadium
Scotch and water!
    a brown hand rubs my balls
Señor you buy me dreenk
    No but how much for you?
    Ten dollars
    Five
    No Señor
    Five
    OK
Ah Señor you have a beeg deek
    ....
Bartender call me a taxi
Si Señor.....
La Posada Motel!
The international bridge, a child slept on the

JT Curran

sidewalk
Are you an American citizen?
YES SIR!
I am a fucking American citizen

Paradise Destroyed

Innocence
        pure and simple
        based on love for fellow man
        bare breasted brown skinned beauties
              skimpering across the sands
              jet black hair blowing in the
              breeze
              bathing in the clear seas
                    giggling
                    and splashing
        strong disease free people
              free people
        dancing and singing in the evening
        loving later
              loving always
Destroyed
        by the god fearing
            bible quoting
            missionary maniacs
        who brought the white man's ways
        to change
              to christianize
                    to ruin
        put a bra on that savage
        clothe their nakedness
        leave your pagan ways
        follow me
              and watch your
                    wonderful civilization
                        DIE

JT Curran

What a day!
    What a day!
Sun melted gray skies
      to blue
    turned to blue
And memories floating past
        floating fast
      at
      Nana's
          house

Beyond the Road

Hey lil bird
    You done met your maker
Hey lil bird
    You gonna meet the scraper
    Scrip scrip scrap
        Scrip scrip scraper
    Gonna let you lie
            til
    You turn to vapor

JT Curran

Justify It Oh Lord

There in the darkness felt
death's blows dealt
to a young man in his prime
who didn't think it time

How to find the justification
as his wife and five kids wait in expectation
for his entrance through the door
that he will open no more

Dinner setting on the stove
prepared by a mother's love
getting blemished from the heat
"Mommy when can we eat?"

"As soon as Daddy arrives home."
And then a ring - the telephone
The mother answers with "Hello"
A pause, anguish, a scream, "Oh no!"

The receiver bounces off the floor
The children too young to know the score
"Mommy can we eat without Daddy tonight?"
"Yes children, I'm sure it will be all right."

Tears fill her eyes, the mother starts to cry
And the kids in their delight
run to the kitchen to be fed
unaware their father's dead

On Sleep

My head hangs heavy
My eyes no longer look
        But wander
                And wonder at the fantasies
Which play upon my mind

I play the role of many
Like an actor
              Blurriness
                    And weariness take their toll
Then my theatre shuts its door

JT Curran

Beyond the Road

IV - PSYCHOLOGICAL PSANDWICHES

Beyond the Road

Beverly
      at 1:00
    for fun?
    to run?
           Who won?
Not the wife
     whose life
Filled with diaper pails
            snips
            and
            snails
and broken nails
            increasingly becomes depressed
          with
           meaningless chores

W   W
 o   o
  n   n
   d   d
    e   e
     r   r
      i   i
       n   n
        g   g
                    Wandering

Bones

They called him Bones
        But I never knew why
        He made me laugh
                And now he's made me cry
                Remembering
        All the times
                I watched him stumble by

"How ya doin young man"
(Sometimes he called me Jake)
He never asked for giving
He never learned to take

He'd squint his eyes
        and bob his head
And draw his lips up tight
Mumbling words of wisdom
He'd vanish in the night

They called him Bones
        And I never asked why
        A nickname from
                Before I was I
                Remembering
        All the times
                I watched him stumble by

Charlie Stearns

His name was Charlie Stearns
And his days were void of yearns
From a lifetime full of burns
And a man who never learns

      When his parents set him free
      At the age of thirty three
      He was never taught to see
      Their protection had a fee

      So the world was full of nice
      As he ventured on the ice
      Like the rolling of the dice
      Filled with dreams and bad advice

Seemed like every job he had
Made him sad or made him mad
Then he'd quit 'cause times were bad
While his brain was shroud in plaid

There was nothing right with life
So he thought he'd take a wife
Unprepared to meet the strife
He slit his wrists to test the knife

      But the job was poorly done
      And when his maker didn't come
      And he'd totaled up the sum
      Seems his search had just begun

So he tried it quite a lot
Taking pains to beat the clock
To keep his world distraught
'Til they kept him and forgot

So now he spends his days
Watching TV matinees
With a schizophrenic gaze
Just a childhood protege

Dr. Shrink

What do you think
    Dr. Shrink
As you sit in your office
    teaching people to live
Reaching for feelings
    You're unable to give
With a pad in your hand
    And one thought in your brain
You pass out prescriptions
    again and again
"If one doesn't work
    try three or four
Keep taking them faithfully
    and I'll give you some more."

What do you think
    Dr. Shrink
As your Zombies come in
    and you keep them alive
With talk of transference
    and all of that jive
Psychological jargon
    mixed with your pills
You capture their wallets
    and capture their wills
"You'll have to keep coming
    for a year maybe more
That's what it takes for an
    analytical cure."

JT Curran

What do you think
    Dr. Shrink
Objectively speaking you
    work on the minds
Of the frightened dependent
    all of those kinds
Of people trapped
    in their shells
Each with their own
    individual hells
"You're my Savior"
    they hope as they fall on their knees
"Help me goddammit
    I'll pay all your fees."

What do you think
    Dr. Shrink
As into each part
    of their lives you delve
When you can't even
    take a good look at yourself
You've removed all your mirrors
    and thrown them away
There's no talk about you
    You've got nothing to say
        Take a shit in the corner
            in a neat little pile
        It stinks Dr. Shrink
            Smell it awhile.

Harold

He never seemed to say
>what was on his mind
He came on soft and warm
>his words were always kind
He had a way of making
>people feel at ease
>While deep inside
>His plans had died
>>And brought him to his knees

He thought he'd be a doctor
>dedicate his self
To helping other people
>who couldn't help themselves
He would have been a good one
>it never did come true
>He lost the start
>Broke his heart
>>And never carried through

He thought he'd be a husband
>investing all his life
Try to start a family
>two children and a wife
Although he almost made it
>something wasn't quite right
>He never gained
>From all the pain
>>And seemed to lose his sight

JT Curran

Like a lost and lonely clown
        with a brightly painted smile
He kept the party going
        crying all the while
The sadness in his eyes
        the pain within his head
    Too much to think
    He had to sink
          And drink his dreams instead

Leighton Sewer

Leighton Sewer the good deed doer
        He liked to help people along
He'd look at himself on the mirrorless shelf
            And dance to the tune of his song
                  Tippy tippy tap
                  Snippy snippy snap
                  Tip Tap Tip Tap Tip Tap
You could go to his bank and before you could thank
            Him for saving your moneyless life
He'd turn on the charm with a flick of his arm
        And sharpen the tip of his knife
                Tippy tippy tap
                Tip Tap Tip Tap Tip Tap
                Snippy snippy snap
A question or two helped enable him to
            Determine how far he could go
He'd send out a shock and pleasantly talk
        About things he couldn't possibly know
                Tip Tap Tip Tap Tip Tap
                Tippy tippy tap
                Snippy snippy snap
And as long as you'd sit lapping up all his shit
            He'd happily give out a loan
But one ill-timed move being out of the groove
            He'd slice up your family and home
                Tip Tap Tip Tap Tip Tap
                Tip Tap Tip Tap Tip Tap
                Tip Tap Tip Tap Tip Tap
                Tip Tap Tip Tap Tip Tap

Peter Calliope

When Peter Calliope
        came to town
The girls would come from miles around
        to hear his music fill the air
        with
        notes of ecstasy everywhere
                anywhere
        He didn't care!

They'd sing
They'd dance
        Drop their pants
        Romp through parks of grassy green
        the notes so soothing so serene
        like
        wingless angels everywhere
                anywhere
        They didn't care!

The rightsters gaped
        and scoffed and sneered
And called the cops to stop the weird
        sounds and skin so bare
        with
        clubs and cuffs everywhere
                anywhere
        They didn't care!

Beyond the Road

Sam S.
        was the best!
But now he spends his time about....
5 years ago
        or maybe 10
And then some more again
        an alcoholic haze
        recalls his golden days
of war
        of holding his breath
        an inch away from sudden death

Remembering
        Remembering
25
    or maybe 30
        Wartime then was not so dirty
    He fucked and fought
        and drank a lot
        While getting caught
        up in the patriotic thing
    To justify
        that he might die
    in a meaningless manner
        and
    no one might remember
    He was a proud and standing member
of Uncle Sam's original Air Force
But
    no one else seems to care
    what he did or where

So
>   on he drinks
>   >   and walks and talks
>   like he did so long ago

What
>   matters?
>   >   Nothing
>   Only gin
>   >   and vodka too
>   to keep his breath from coming through
>   denying that he's had a few
>   >   too many
>   >   too long
>   >   >   to change
>   his VFW warped mind

Suffering
Suffering
Suffering

Beyond the Road

The devil came to Carl that night
    when shadows cast their eerie light
        that made him shake
           and bake
                with fright
He saw things he'd never seen
    of how to make the world so clean

He listened to his beating heart
    to give the signal when to start
        to shock and scare
           and tear
                apart
All the people on the earth
    who helped to cheat him of his worth

As he drifted from the haze
    wondering where he'd been for days
        and why the pain
           his brain
                ablaze
And why his eyes were full of tears
    and why his life was void of years

His body sank beneath the weight
    he felt his mind evaporate
        mixed with mud
           and blood
                and hate

JT Curran

While seven people fell to hell
   he slept
        the devil's sentinel

The Secretary of Perjury

Ladies and Gentlemen
The Secretary of Perjury
The Honorable Ronald McDonald
    Ahem............

        I'd like to take this moment
        To spread a few more lies
        Governmental pies from me
        To smack between your eyes

We've been working on a subtle change
To make you all believe
The bullshit that we're handing out
The weird things we conceive

We hope to have it operating
In a month or two
We've got to work the bugs out
And administrate the crew

        We need to train on double talk
        And truth must be forgotten
        We're screening all the applicants
        Who have no piss to pot in

With a little bit of luck
And a lot of overtime
We hope that this new agency
Will take the place of crime

JT Curran

We know that we can do it
We know what you deserve
You're the ones we have to thank
We're only here to serve

                              Thank you

Beyond the Road

JT Curran

**V - OBSERVATIONS
& OBSTACLES**

Beyond the Road

Hey Johnny boy
Ya made it big
    sang your song
    danced your jig
    whistled wide
    whistled far
    made yourself a superstar
Wonder
    what
        you think you are
Money bulging at the seams
Pockets lined with fractured dreams
      Round and round in limousines
      Round and round in limousines

Snow bound
Home bound
World is round
    round and round
    yesterday's songs
    yesterday's longs
Vinyl discs spinning sounds
    of a missing
        generation
    Stealing kisses
as parental feet pace the
        distance
of our dreams
    Hot Heavy
    Dripping desires
    Oozing cross carpets
        of newly decorated cellars
Cheek to cheek
Week to week
    Waiting wanting
        wanting
            Wanting

Beyond the Road

Exit
    Stage right
    Fleeing from the moment
    Fleeing from the night
Apprehension
    Tension
    Did I forget to mention
All the fears
    the choking fears
that shake my bedtime fantasies
    and keep them
        out of sight

JT Curran

A little ripple
      through the ranks
  Many pleases
  Many thanks
        Titter Tatter
        Pitter Patter
Hey man, what's the matter
  Sure would like to hear from you
  Hear your plan
  See your view
      Maybe have a beer or two
      Hey man,
           What's new?

Beyond the Road

With trembling heart
    I rush
        rush
            rush
What are they doing?
Oh
    how I love to watch them
        interact
        moving
        learning
    totally involved with the
        world
            of things
    totally involved

Gabriel

Gabriel, come blow your horn for me
        come meet the dawn with me
                Endlessly
                      You gotta see
Gabriel,
    come get it on with me

Gabriel, play a little tune for me
        come see the moon with me
                Sailing free
                Wailingly
Gabriel,
    won't you croon for me

Gabriel, won't you sing a song for me
        come feel the warmth from me
                Tenderly
                    It's time to be
Gabriel,
    come blow your horn for me

Mr. Jones
      Mr. Jones
You done turned them into bones
        Took them from their homes
        Made them into clones
And amid the wails and moans
Mr. Jones
      Mr. Jones
You done turned them into stones

JT Curran

Disaster
      Disaster
Someone should have asked her
    if
        she'd
            mind having her
          body
      dashed against the wall

Beyond the Road

Yo Brian
        Thought you'd changed
Not quite so mentally deranged
Got it together
        and all that jazz
        Well.....
Yo Brian
        Where is you as

JT Curran

Reminiscing again
History lessons on old port towns
Hey man
    I must be twelve again
And here he is
Bathing in nostalgia
    Regimented moments
        in time
Like the last 25 years
    have come to an end
6:45 on a Sunday morning
I must be crazy
Captain Alcohol
    begins his
        long
            journey
A quick prayer
    insanity
    profanity
    and most of all
        anonymity
2 lost souls
kneeling
    in worlds apart
Jesus,
    I must be twelve again
The bakery!
    another ritual
    soon to be broken
    by fate's iron grip

Beyond the Road

Ah yes
    fresh baked bread
    the
        aroma
    brings back more memories
And the pain man
I keep feeling all this pain
See that chimney
        Oh yea
    Woosh!
I had a warm ass
        then
Ah he was quite a man
Spanning
a lifetime
    into a few minutes
Round the town
Up and down
    Storm's a coming
Yea man
    I feel it
What the fuck am I doing
        on this trip
I know
    I'm twelve again!
Just bear with me for a few more
            minutes
Spare a few minutes for an old
            drunk
Yea
    the alcohol is ever present

    slowly closing in
just another mile or two
      What?
    What's the message?
Could I really be
          twelve again
His perceptions never change
Always right
His deceptions
              not so strange
Cause
      he's really full of fright
Now,
     Here it comes
A casual mention
        of
       Korea!?
Never,
     I mean never have I heard this
And man
     let me tell you
     I've heard all his stories
     at least
     at the very least
     All
     One hundred times
Korea?
   Yea, I was stunned
   He was recalled
That's when your uncle kind of
   turned chicken shit

Beyond the Road

```
          [Chicken Shit!]
           [Kind of]
             This
              is
getting heavy
And then,
           Subject's changed
He's told me something
           significant
                    I think
Maybe
     that I'll always
          be
       twelve again
And
Maybe
     that's all he's
          ever
          been
```

JT Curran

Ackley
    Ackley
Be right backly
        aptly primed
Ya man,
    I called him John
    the man with the super duper hard on
            aptly rhymed
He'd return each year
    hand on beer
    doing all those crazy things
        he was famous for
"Ackley
    Ackley"
    the crowd roared on
    his mind
Confused?
Amused?
    used and used
Each year
    another binge
    another cringe
        inch and inch
        upon his waist
His life more space
Physically speaking
His wife lost grace
    lost face

Beyond the Road

And
    Ackley
        Ackley
        went right backly

JT Curran

Kentucky Derby
        Herbie
Meet ya there
        Sprawling
        Balling
        Overhauling
                hoards
Crowded together for
        One
        Glorious
        Moment
        In
        Time

Watergate
>Watergate
What's a matter Mate
>Late
>Late
>>Make a break
>>For heaven's sake
>>Whatcha gonna take
Water's
>Leaking through the gate

Running
> from the mailbox
> with his little fist
>> tightly
> wrapped around the letters
Smiling
> Waving
>> Yelling
>>> "Look Dad,
We got mail!"

Beyond the Road

The king of bebop passed away
I heard his heart stopped yesterday
        I think
        He sunk
But,
    what became of the Monk

Just keeps getting
          worse Johnny boy
Just when you think
      you have the world
        by the balls
Just when you think
      all's well
Just when - then
Some cocksucker
      tells you
        you have bad breath

Beyond the Road

JT Curran

VI - DEPRESSION CITY
WHEW! 77 IN REVIEW

Beyond the Road

Hey Clay
        Whatta ya say
Done some nipping today ?
Little sipping as they say
                They?
    Whatever happened to they
    Your wife
    Your kids
Never seems to matter
When you're on the skids
      Aimlessly walking
                  To this point or that
      Aimlessly talking
                  Where are you at
Hey Clay:
      Where the fuck are you?

JT Curran

Quebec City

Fabled gables
    neatly tucked
        in triangular arrays
Equilateral, they stretch
    in all directions
        Dotted
        Spotted
        Planes of existence
  Sliced by shallow rivers
      they gather in momentum
       'til the mountains meet the city
In a grand display of old and new
New ideas to exploit the old
And old ideals
    to keep uptight visions
        in
          the
      back of one's mind

Depression Seventy Seven

Where does one start? How does one begin?
        Start where one ends
        Start with the sin
Depression
        so full of expression
                Confession
so full of depression
        Lesson
    so full of confusion
     (less than amusing)
        nothing to learn
         and nowhere to turn
Here we go round the mulberry bush
        the mulberry bush
        the mulberry bush
Here we go round
Here we go
       Here we
       Here we
       Here we
              Here
              Here

JT Curran

Oh the things you could've done
    writing like you do
        Mr. Rimbaud

All those hearts you could've won
    you rascal you
        dontcha know

But you never realized
    the extent
        to which you went

Wouldn't mother be surprised
    at the dent
        you never meant

Beyond the Road

What's going on?
        From dusk 'til dawn
In the street
        And on the lawn
  Got to listen to the news
  Listen to another's views
  Make them mine and refuse
  To deal with the frightened you's

What's happening?
        From dawn 'til dark
Throughout the world
        And in the park
  Got to see the big events
  Forming thoughts from their comments
  Teetering on a picket fence
  Wondering why I feel so tense

Whatcha been up to
        During the day
While you're working
        While you play
  Got to hear the latest rumor
  Lift me with a little humor
  All the garbage I deplore
  Wondering
        how can I
                endure

JT Curran

A very good gesture
                we offer to you
Eleven remains
                of people you knew
And all that remains
                a handful of dust
                  just want you to trust
                      we
                  don't have seventy more
Just want to be friends
Making amends!
Ah, don't feel so sad
You weren't beaten that bad
                Look on the board at the score!
          (of course if you lied
            And inflated your side
              To cover your hide)
                then
A very good gesture
                we offer to you
Eleven remains
                of people you knew

Beyond the Road

One Two Three
        Whatta ya see
Step right up   Step right up
        What'll it be
          One for the road
          and two for the tree
Three
      magically speaking
      makes everything free

His words were
    lost
before they came
               fragments
like lightning
              fractured
      through the rain
   again
   again
         he wracked his brain
And like the soap suds down the drain
He hung on dearly all the same
            And
checked his wallet for his name

Beyond the Road

Words
    commun
        i
      cate
No
  not
  what
  one
  is
    trying
        to
      say
Only
    what
    one
    is
      trying
        to
      feel

The verge
>   The surge
>   Oh the surge!
>   The urgeless wordless flight
>   fleeing in the morning
>   feeling in the night

On the rim
>   The brim
>   Oh the brim!
>   The dim-lit friendless edge
>   feeling for the flooring
>   fleeing from the ledge

Beyond the Road

JT Curran

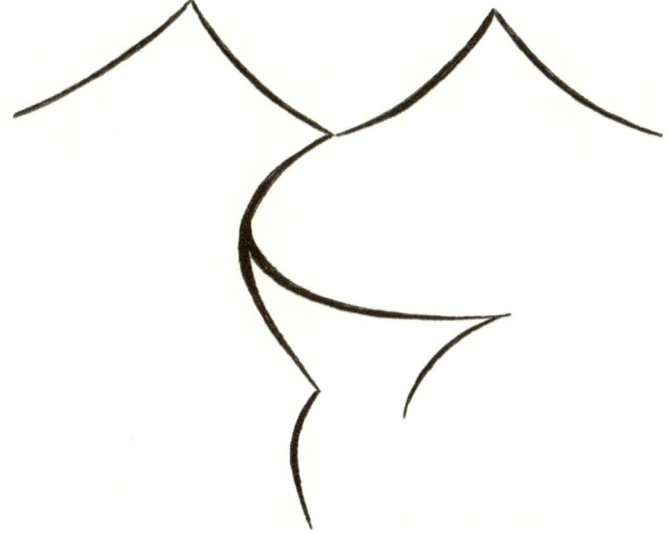

VII - FLYING WITHOUT WINGS

Beyond the Road

Oh
    those eyes
Looking
       longing
for some unknown thing
for some unknown reason
they draw me
like a painful magnet

Watching
    your models
Smoking
       chattering
in soap opera language
making it up
juicing it up
You keep silent
half smiling
the magnet gets stronger

Spending
    your life
You see me
    out of the corner
of your unmoving eye
wondering what I have to offer
to you - to the women
to the magnet
    to that binding
       chunk of steel

Big tits
    flopping
Bouncing
    erotic jello
           ass wiggling
           jello
And me
Trying to be a gentleman
       A Gentle Man
Fighting the fears
    of chauvinism
Find myself
    mildly amused
    mildly aroused
        and lookin'
        for the whipped cream

Budding little girl
   Your petals
   Slowly unfolding

Painful little girl
   You're growing
   Faster than I can stand
   Faster than I
            want to believe
           Your petals
     Unfolding
Budding little girl

JT Curran

She smiles
        She laughs
Life oozing through her pores
        Bouncing down
        The hall
A lease on life
That most of us
        would dearly pay

Beyond the Road

I sense the fear
as your life
        begins
to unfold
        into chunks
       of your own
doing

I know the fear
and wish I could share
        the feeling
But
    I couldn't stand the pain

Terrorist
You kill
    the dreams of others
    creating nightmares
You dream
    of what?
    Freedom!
    Your own chunk of sand
Hey man
    What do you want?
    You've got my attention
But it only makes me angry
      and
        I feel like killing you
Not the effect you wanted?
    You got a mission
          my man
It sure ain't love we're talking about

Beyond the Road

History in the making
Hulkamania
    in Hartford
    as the long haired muscle clown
    does his act
Screaming fans
Releasing emotions
That were much better spent
    believing in Santa Claus

JT Curran

Before Kids
    Debts
        Mortgages
           And the daily bullshit
There was
    us

Beyond the Road

Winter snows and
    wood piles
Melting away with the thoughts
      of Spring
Longer days
      Thoughts of flesh
      Visible again
Pushes one's mind
To the limits of yesterday
And the last time I saw your
      body

Sweeping snows
        and red sunsets
Over that ridge is Heaven
Over that ridge is Nirvana
And I feel elated
        that it's so
            close

Butterball
   The pre-basted Turkey
You stretch your arms
And roll across the floor
Reaching
        for acceptance
Reaching
        for love
Reaching
        for anything
        But the loneliness
              You feel

JT Curran

I saw you standing by the
                  gas pumps
Belly bulging
      with future plans
Boyfriend wiping the windshield
You avoiding my eyes
As if to say
        We may not be happy
           But at least we can fuck

Beyond the Road

I drove across that bridge
A lot of times
    And up that washed out
                    road
    Late at night
    Black as Satan's heart
    No flashlight
The road was the excitement
The bridge was just sitting there
A way to get across the river
    and a short cut to home

Raise the flags
       and jump for joy
Another
       ordinary event
         turned to an
            extravaganza
The cameras crackle
      The fires
         of patriotism
           burn in splendor
It's
   Half time

Beyond the Road

No privacy!
        No privacy!
Next to ecstacy
Next to silently
        Quietly
                She said to me
                No privacy!

JT Curran

The years pass by
    Quicker
      than you can remember
That place
With the rain chains
When we walked around
    So boldly
      Pretending
          We knew
          All
          The answers

Beyond the Road

My world
        turns
        slow enough as is
But when
        you're down
        It
        Stops
And I feel like
        I'm
            gonna
                fall
                    off

JT Curran

Walking down the path
    To the trailer
    Cigarette
          dangling
    Puffin' up a storm
Kicking toys out of the way
    End of the day
    End of the week
        Can't wait to pop
        that first beer

Beyond the Road

Alone
    Lying in bed
I mean alone
    Not metaphysically
        Speaking
Just me
    and my thoughts
    filled with you
Wondering
    Why I toss and turn
      and
    can't get to sleep

JT Curran

Iron Ann
The queen of ice
She'd fuck you
    in a minute
Over
    that is
'Cause I don't think
    the juices have been
    flowing for 20 years

Beyond the Road

Cold
    So cold and lonely
Melancholia
    Strikes
        like a baseball bat
      between
          the eyes
And you're
    gone
Dealing with your
    own pain
      Alone

JT Curran

It's just a phase
                You're going through
Let it pass
Let it go
      flow
      with the wisdom of age
Why in 2 or 3 years you'll have
      forgotten all

Beyond the Road

Sometimes
The thought of your smile
Is the only thing
That keeps me
        Going

JT Curran

Beyond the Road

JT Curran

VIII - REFLECTIONS & INTERJECTIONS

Beyond the Road

I woke up in a different world
    Laughter gone
    Somber songs
           filled the air
           with feelings
  I was unfamiliar with

I woke up
    And didn't know where I was
    I breathed in and out
    wondering
        what it was I did

Doing felt hollow
    Hollow felt lonely
    Lonely felt gone
    Something was missing
and
I woke up

JT Curran

Paste his picture on
    the screen
Posed with guns
    looking mean
32's
    the score to beat
Get ready
    makers meet
The next
    great
        gunslinger
Steps
    to the plate

Florida - April 2007

The birds
   were everywhere
   walking
   wading
   warily looking
         over their shoulders
   watching
   waiting
   wondering what
         the fuck was going on

The people
   were everywhere
   walking
   wiping
   water from their brows
         sweating bullets
   watching
   waiting
   wondering what
         the fuck was going on

JT Curran

The turkeys are horny
    Struttin' their stuff
    Feathers fanned
    Facing the truth
That
      no matter what you do
      no matter how you look
You ain't getting nothing
      'til she says
Go for it, Big Boy

Beyond the Road

The scales
        tip
The world slips
        into
                disarray
The day
        trips
      Stumbling
        along
            the lost
                weekends
The bend
          ends
       just around
            the corner
And
    nothing
        makes sense
            anymore

JT Curran

That smirky little smile
   Out of the corner
   Your mouth
   Gives you away
Like a wanted poster

Beyond the Road

Something
        missing
I don't have
    enough ammo
    when
        the hordes
Come charging
    through
    the
        countryside

JT Curran

Watch the money
 pile up
 one thin bill
  on another
How
 many inches
  do you
   want

Beyond the Road

It's me
   always has been
My mind
   says one thing
My body
   does the
         other

It's me
   always has been
My deeds
   don't match
My fetes
   grow with
         age

It's me
   always has been
My thoughts
   my oughts
My nots
   keep me
         saying
It's me
Always has been

Paris

Hey Paris
   Where you gonna be?
   when
        all of a sudden
        no one gives a shit
                anymore

Hey Paris
   Where you gonna go?
   when
        the assholes wake up
        and look for new
                coverage

Hey Paris
   I heard they named
   a city after you
   Guess....
   I was wrong
            Oops!

Beyond the Road

Erectile dysfunction
    Gonna meet you
        at the junction
    and
            by Jesus
    If you don't get hard
You'll
      have more than
                ED

JT Curran

You bitch
    complain
and
    everything's
    a major fucking problem
Your look
    on life
Is
    misplaced
    a major fucking problem
Your head
    lost in space
Or
    somewhere
    on another fucking planet
Wake up
    Asshole
You
    just might
    make something of yourself

Beyond the Road

The
Lord of dance
     made
        his final leap
Tapping across
     the floor
     with the
        assurance of a
             leprechaun
Peering
     over his shoulder
Dance my lad
     Dance
        'Til you can dance no more
Then
    Take a rest
        You've earned it

JT Curran

"There ain't nuthin'
    like a good piss"
Don would say
    pissing off the porch
    into the snow
        mud
       grass
           whatever the season
Outdoors
   That's where a good
      piss
ought to be

Beyond the Road

The hills are alive
    with the sound of
        construction
Once great
    fields and trees
    sloped to the valleys
        and streams
Green and vibrant
Now
    Ty-par and piles of gravel
    make the way
for more people
    to park their cars
    and demand
    sewers
        internet connections
    snow plows
        electricity
and a shitload
    of shopping centers
Dontcha think
    it looks a whole
        lot better?

Been there
    Done that
        Gone

Been there
    Done that
        So long

Been there
    Done that
        Man!

Been there
    Done that
        Understand?

Ain't nothing
    Gonna make me
        pay
            attention

Beyond the Road

Are you living in fear
                  dear?
Waiting
       for one disaster
          after another
Watching
         the skies for telltale
            clouds
Working
         the crowd for
             a reading
Temperature's rising
        no one's paying
              attention

JT Curran

The garden
        Gone
        Lawn
                Replaced
The once
        Luscious
        Vegetables
Stood as proud
as the grower

The Grower
        Gone
        Down
              Under

The earth
        Ashes
        To dust
The soil welcomed him
    with a smile

Beyond the Road

There ain't
    no rides
        at the
                Common Ground
                    Fair
There ain't
    no sugar
        at the
                Common Ground
                    Fair
There ain't
    no caffeine
        at the
                Common Ground
                    Fair
There ain't
    no smoking
        girly shows
        or
        games of chance
        at the
                Common Ground
                    Fair
How fair is that?

The big bang
    did its thing
And
    all of a sudden
Some
    billions and billions
    of years later
    we came into being
Must
    have been the hand
        of god
Who else
    could wait that long

Beyond the Road

I felt
    the urge
to call you up
    strong
        urge
            it was
Was
    too bad
        the urge
        will always
            be
      just
        an urge

Woke up this morning
        and
                my dick was gone
Must be getting old
        can't remember
        where or when
                I last used it
Viagra
        didn't help
Hard to fuck
        without a dick
Spirit
        willing indeed
No tube
        for the seed

Beyond the Road

You
    talk about
    tsunamis
Old age
One moment
      you're
           surfing along
Next
     you're
        sitting in a bar
            wondering

Sign me up!
    Bomb vest
    Blow myself
        into a billion
                atoms
For some
    crazy fucker
    with hatred
        in his
            eyes
Yeah
    I'm sure
        Allah
            is waiting
Don't
    Hold your breath
               Dick head

Beyond the Road

At least
    the American
        women
Have
    bigger tits
    than
        the Chinese
That
    should
        help with
          a perfect
            ten point 0
After all
    It's a game
        of inches

Gathering shit
    Like a fucking
        Pack rat
We collect
    Things
    For dissemination
        To our heirs
    Fight
    For the right
        To collect things
This was my mother's
        my father's
        my grandmother's
        my pile of shit
            Grows
Can memories be that
        shallow?

Beyond the Road

The hearse
      rolled on the icy road
      snow piled on the side
      People
           lined up
           like a parade
The body
      inside the flag-draped coffin
      rolled on the icy road
      People
           somber
           some crying
The hero
      because he died for a cause
      rolling on the icy road
      People
           feeling bad
           in silence
Ironic
      Silence
           is what
                  placed
                      him
                          there!

The nice things
        The little things
        Things
We do
        Things
We get
            for the ones
We care about

The nice thoughts
        The little thoughts
        Thoughts
We have
        Thoughts
We get
            about the ones
We care about

Thoughts
Things
        ?

Beyond the Road

Time was
    Time is
    Passing
          like a runaway
                freight train

Time is
    Time was
    Lasting
          for an instant
            Maybe
            Memories
Are all we are

JT Curran

Crazy!
    You wanna see
           crazy?
Step in my shoes
    For a while
      The view
          is incredible

Beyond the Road

Memorial Day
    Cloudy
        Overcast
        Indy over
            600 too
Just movie
    after movie
    second rate
          war flicks
No sun
    to suck me
          outside
Just a
    notion
that
    somewhere
      sometime
        someone
          died
In a war
      Remember?

Emily
    Won't you come outside
Emily
    They're coming far and wide
    Please
They want to hear
    Let's have a beer
      Talk out loud
    and meet the crowd
      Man
          You would have wowed
        the fuck
          out of 'em

Beyond the Road

Assisted living
    Like a prison
        Without walls
Nowhere to go
    Can't remember anyway
How 'bout
    somebody wheeling
      me down
        to the smoking
          area
Hey
  I need some
      assistance
        here

JT Curran

Helicopter time
    Sweeping the land
        for the green
Those
    pointed leaves
        that cause so
            much damage

Beyond the Road

JT Curran

IX - MOSTLY 9

Beyond the Road

Whenever I hear
        Upholsterer
I think of Sandy
Doo-wopping in the store front
                window
The Violators
        Harmonizing
Sandy banging the drums
And the old man listening
        always listening
                and
      Warping his son's mind
      Like a sorcerer
      From Hell

JT Curran

Danny Boy
   I knew
        you didn't have
           it in you
Nothin' left
   to blow across
       the Atlantic
I knew
    you were
        already
Out of breath
But still
    I wanted to see
         you

Beyond the Road

The Sunday crowd
    Beaming white
    Teeth so perfect
        they could be a commercial
Children
    like robots
        sit and eat
Cause
    you know
    what'll happen
        if you
            misbehave
You'll
    burn
        in
            Hell

Coming back
      from church
      full of Jesus
Riding the center line
    with a big ass
             SUV
Get out of the way
        fucker
I'm on a mission
    and
        breakfast
        is just around
           the corner

Beyond the Road

Remember
      the future
When the past
      brought
           peace
           love
           and
                happiness
                    forever

P. J.
    Met his maker
      Not a mover
        nor shaker
          A simple man
          with holy blood
Who walked
    the path
      of St. Francis
    in the mud
    of Millinocket

Beyond the Road

She
    walks in
        the cafeteria
Duty bound
    discomfort
        on her face
Her mother-in-law
    asleep
        at the table
Dirty deed done
    She
        turns
        quickly
            out the door

JT Curran

My hero
   a jibbering
    jabbering
        mess
of alcoholic
   haze
     and
       lost
         thoughts
as
  the world
     passed
       him by
Looking
    looking
       looking
Unable to grasp
    his demons
        in the end

Beyond the Road

Compromise
     I surmise
Is
    just a matter
      of
     words

JT Curran

Sitting
        easy chair
        behind the counter
Smoking
        watching
        the cars go by
Nipping
        a glass
        beneath
           the vision of others
Lost in thought
        waiting
           for the next
               customer
Remembering
        awful
           thoughts
               from
                   Vietnam

Beyond the Road

Sagging
      tits
      swaying
      left right
Wrinkled tattoos
    Old and worn
      like the
        gray beards
White people
      dancing
  as only white people
             can
Slight coastal breeze
  in the hot sun
Must be
    the Blues Festival

JT Curran

Make your
            move
                    baby
Time is
        short
And
    who knows
        how you'll
                feel
                    in
            an hour

Dr. Chuck
    ran out of luck
        plucked
His soul
    in a non-conventional
    way
        Hey
Sorry to hear
    I kind of
        liked him
    in a real
        conventional
    way

JT Curran

Collateral
    that's what I feel
        like
Damage
    Waiting to happen
'Cause
    When the shit
        comes down
Invisible
    Collateral
        Damage
          is what
        I'll
          be

Beyond the Road

    He likely
            died
                    from exposure
    Exposure
             to what
                  no job
                  no thoughts
                  no future
        likely
              He sure
                    as hell did

JT Curran

```
Sanderlings
    Skittering
            along
Making room
      for the
              Tern Stones
While his
      majesty
              the Royal
Turns his head
      from side
         to side
              in
                 approval
```

Beyond the Road

The streetlight
   Eerie
      snow blowing
         like fog
            in a London
               movie
Must be
    2 feet
  No way in hell
    we're getting
       to the airport
No fucking
      way
Like a ghost
   An apparition
Dad says
    "That's a Marine
     I can tell by the way
     he's walking."
Danny's
    Home

JT Curran

I
deleted you
    from
        my speed dial
Feel the pain?
Fuck you
    Asshole

Beyond the Road

The father
      knows it all
     lecturing
        on the finer
           points of
       catching a pass
Hey son
     Catch the
         fucking ball
And
   just maybe
  you can be
    as good
      as your
        old man

JT Curran

The bar
    like all bars
    or some bars
      well,
    the bars
        I used to hang
            around
Was filled
    with some
    of the loneliest
      people
   in the
      world
        at least
the world
      I used to hang
        around

Beyond the Road

The problem
    Is
        We've been watching
            the world
            in 2-D
        For the past 50
                    years
Now they're
      going to give us
           another
                  dimension
Won't be long
    We'll be back
           to Normal

JT Curran

All that
       dancing
Seems like
      You shouldn't
           be so
               fat

Beyond the Road

Perspectives
Lunch counter diplomats
On twisted stools
      schools
        of thought
          fools
       of naught
Ambassadors of the world
Solving the problems
While waiting
    for their muffins

JT Curran

The apple fell
   or
      did the earth
         jump up
             to meet it
The gravity
   of
      the situation
   is
      much too much
            to comprehend

Beyond the Road

The sun
      fades
Grayness
      turns to dark
The night
      surrounds us
Blackness
      one by one
          the stars
              break through
Twinkling
      like they's sposed to

JT Curran

Whispering
Words of wisdom
      The old man coughed
      Looked around
And slipped back
      into his own reality

Beyond the Road

Mostly money she said
I mean
       What else is there?

JT Curran

Beyond the Road

JT Curran

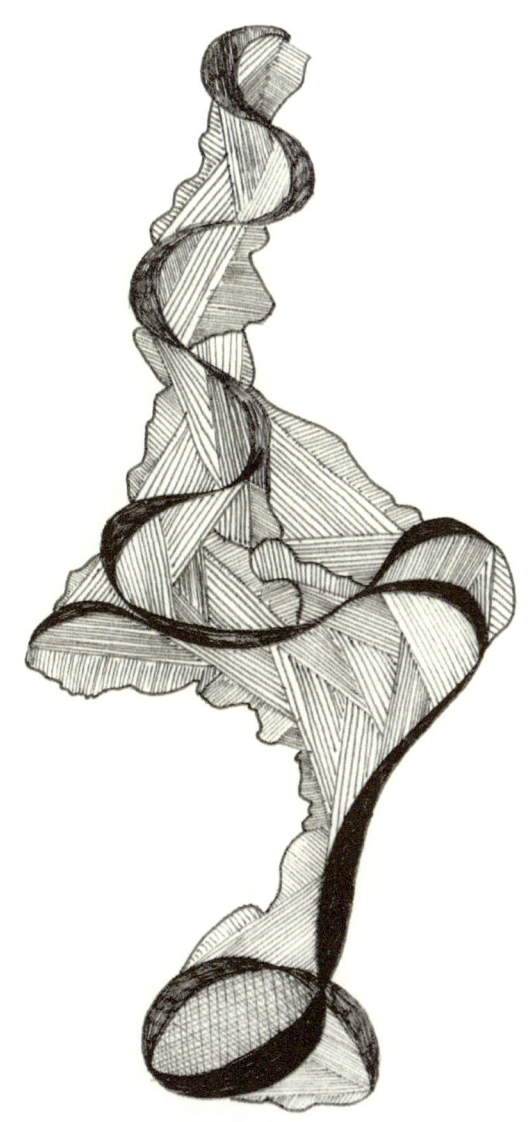

X -HODGEPODGE, OLIO AND OTHER SCRAPS

Beyond the Road

Buffalo
      Bill coding
      Dialing
            for dollars
Why don't you drop by
         with your
               checkbook

JT Curran

Ya ever notice
      that cashews
      look like
           commas,
                    Huh?

Beyond the Road

   Sun shining
      School waning
      You run to the car
         Shoeless
         Eating a Ring Ding
         or some other nutritious
         snack
      Off the porch
        like you're flying
          Hell!
              You are flying
       Only touching ground
         to satisfy the onlookers

JT Curran

Stalking round the room
Looking cool
      Oh so cool
    Handshake
        Smile
            A few words here
            A few words
There
          A few
Nods
    Seeking out your next victim

Beyond the Road

Expensive suits
    Polished words
Out of my element
      again
Keep your cool
      drool
        and show a hint
          of
        arrogance

My whiteness
      Your darkness
Enthralled
We balled
      Entangled
      Black & white
      Gray area

Beyond the Road

Another hero
        Comes to the light
        Start the camera
        Shine the brights
        Praise the lord
        and, let's
                delve into
                  any
                peaceful minute
                    this poor fucker
                      might have
                          had
Hey
    someone's
        bound to find
            something wrong

We watched........
      The deer pawed
          through the snow
      Apples
        the mission
The moon full
      Casting eerie
           shadows
    Unaware
         that
We watched
      The deer paw

Beyond the Road

The boxes lined
    like
    leaflets waiting
to be distributed
    from us to you
        bodies
young men no more

JT Curran

I thought I was teaching you
   but
I learn more from you
   than books and texts
   and booze and sex
   and lots of subtitles
      with hip language
that leaves me wondering
     wandering
        through the throes of life

Beyond the Road

Used to be
    Cold was cold
Now
    it's bitter, brutal, bone chilling
    Wind chill
    Colder than a witch's tit
        in the Klondike
Words
    that shiver the psyche
    and stiffens the bones
Wishing for a warmer forecast

JT Curran

Don't know much
    about St. Joe
    He was kind of reclusive
        you know
        or maybe
    He just didn't get
        the headlines

Beyond the Road

I remember
     walking across the sands
     Willard Beach
     the dark pavilion
     Little Richard blasting
The jukebox
     Looking like a creature from
            outer space
     Hooked up to the only outlet
            in the place
     Sucking what little electricity
            we had in those days
And always 2 girls jitterbugging
            in bathing suits
            dancing on boards
            worn thin from
            thousands of bare feet
Buy a popsicle
     and put a nickel in the slot
Anything
     to keep the girls dancing

JT Curran

Somewhat like Caesar
with one minor difference
        She came
        She saw
        She squandered

To Donald

Friday
        Afternoon
        tank thinking
            drinking
Moscow Mules
Twist of lime
        Time -
      less fools
          fools for love
We talked
        shared
            dared
To let ourselves be
Free

And you
        the catalytic converter
        chugging along
        like nothing's wrong
You wink
        You laugh
        (Oh that infectious laugh)
And make me smile
        Even though I didn't want to

JT Curran

Too bad you're
    such an asshole
But then
    could anyone so perfect
        be less

Beyond the Road

JT Curran

XI -SPLITTING WOOD AND OTHER MINDLESS TASKS

Beyond the Road

Chomped
    Cigar stub
Sticking out
        of the corner
        of his mouth
Retired
    Deputy Sheriff
Watching the muddy water
Can't see
    any fish
But
    keeps looking anyway
Who knows
    maybe God
        will clear
            things up

JT Curran

Ripples
    on the white sand
Sun
    sucking the
        whiteness
            from my skin
Little heron
   strolls across
   the beach
     like
       he owns it

Beyond the Road

Lined up
    slurping
        ice cream
Like pigs
    at the trough
The family
    makes plans
Hope there's a Target
        nearby
Oh yeah
    No problem
Slop up the rest
    and
We'll waddle
    down the
        road

JT Curran

Ya
  been down
  down
     in the dark
dark
    mines
Where the gasses
      choke
          canaries
And
   explode
      with just a mention
      of spark
Hey
  have ya
  been
     down

Beyond the Road

Doing
    Nothing
        The world
            goes by
                bye
                    bye
Sitting
    On my ass
Wondering
    What
What to do next
    The list
        All the things
            I've wanted
            waited
            yearned
                to do
Fuck it
    I'll do something
        tomorrow

JT Curran

Sheer White
    Summer type dress
Clinging
    to beautiful
        skin
Smile
    shining
Like she was in the stands
    at the Kentucky Derby
Nice tats
    I thought
And
    nice tits
        too

Beyond the Road

The hills
     of Western Maryland
     rolling
          giant swells
              of prehistoric
                  waves
Right
     around Frostburg
An open I-beam
     Noah's Ark
     Sits
Waiting for donations
     and
        the next
            great flood

JT Curran

Driving around
   Not so aimlessly
     Maybe
16 oz PBR between
         the legs
Checking out
    Changes
       Been awhile
         since
You've been here
     Cloudy - blustery
      Not much else to do
Hey
    Wouldn't one of them
      red hot dogs
      make the trip
          special
Took ten stops
     and three beers
before we finally found
       one
Mustard
   relish
      onions
         steamed roll
Nostalgia
   has its limits
     but
This time
    we hit the
      jackpot

Beyond the Road

Persistence
      and
           Patience
Pays off

JT Curran

(Cuatro de Mayo)

5 billion
        years ago
The sun
        began
                to light up
                        the Earth
After many tries
        life
                crept out
                      of the soup
              into the landscape
Only took 4.98

Indiscretions
    Time and
        again
Can't seem
    to keep
        it in your
            pants
What's
    a couple of kids
    out of wedlock
Hey,
    I was only
        fucking
            around

JT Curran

Won't be long
    before everyone
        knows what everyone
            else is doing
Standing
    Driving
        Sitting
            Know what
                I'm doing now
Yeah
    you're missing
        the world
        passing
        like
            a bullet
through glass

Gospel
    According to Mary
Magdeline, that is
    Jesus' confidante
        One he loved the most
        One who held his hand
      Washed his feet
        And made him feel
          like a man
He told her
    the truth
      and
    nothing but the truth
      and yet
        we
Don't hear
    much about her
      these days
She'd a made
    a great
      Pope

JT Curran

Parables
    and
        metaphors
What's with
        all the secret
            shit
Why don't you
        just come
            out with it
You know
        The Truth
  I'm
      getting tired
            of guessing

Breaking up
    like the clouds
        they say
Breaking up
    like a relationship
        gone astray
Breaking up
    like a funny
        story
Breaking up
    like the waves
        on the rocks
Breaking up
    opposite
        of
            Breaking down

Just wondering
      how
            many cops
Are
    itching
To blow
      some
            poor motherfucker
To
  Kingdom
          Come
Seems
      The times
         are
             changing
                  again

Ran
    into Mighty Mouse
        today
            At the Folk Festival
Thought he was
        long gone
Age hasn't
        been his friend
I doubt
        he can get off
            the ground now
Anyway
        his cape was
            missing
No way
        he was going
            to save
                the day

JT Curran

The swamp
    frozen
Tire burning
    in the middle
  acrid
       warmth
And there you were
    an angel
         on ice
So Graceful
    I forgot
        you were
  dressed
       in winter's garb
My heart
    triple lutzed
        and axeled
Mesmerized
    by your eyes
       in the dark

Beyond the Road

Time to
      store the feeders
The hummingbirds
    gone
        on their way
            to South America
The hawk
      family left
        a few weeks ago
The deer
    are eating
        the beet tops
          tomatoes
        beans
          and whatever pleases
            their fancy
The fuckers never helped
      with the planting
          or weeding
Our gourmet garden
    reduced
        to
a ruminant
      smorgasbord
Anger aside
  the air seems
      like menthol
The leaves
  are looking around
    for color
And the woodpile

JT Curran

    begs for cover
Thank god
        it's football
                season

Beyond the Road

Reality
   reduced to prime time
      contrivances
Looking
   for things
      to occupy empty
         minds
Entertainment
   for lost
      souls
Meanwhile
   the seasons change
    water flows
      down falls, streams, rivers
       amidst
         the mountains
and valleys
     and
just maybe
   a touch
    of
      Reality

JT Curran

Daze
    Days
Wondering
     where I am
     what I'm doing
        how I got here
and
     where I'm going
Down
   the hall
      and to the left
Don't
   forget
     to wash your
          hands
    It's dinner
       time

Beyond the Road

They're
        dropping like flies
Old
        heroes, friends,
                enemies
And
        shitloads
        of the greatest
                generation
Like a WWII
        bombing run
          over Germany
But
        none of these
        are coming
            back

JT Curran

Dressed in camo
    Hand in hand
        the young couple
    Hopelessly
          in love
Walking
    down the street
Wonder
    how they found
        each other

Beyond the Road

Have you noticed
    College cheerleaders
      seem to have
      smaller tits
          these days
Sign of the times
But
    the pros
Implant City
    Cleavage
      Now
          isn't that
            what football's
            all
              about

JT Curran

Weather
      patterns
Kind of like
  a wave
       rolling up the
            sand
     recedes
       and before you
        know it
     another one
       takes its place
The calm
    before the storm
The dark
    before the dawn
Just
   another
      fucking
         snow storm

Beyond the Road

Snow
    Like in a globe
    Slowly
    Dropping
        to the ground
Quiet
   If you
       couldn't see it
You
    wouldn't know
        it was
           there

JT Curran

Facebook
    Took a piss
        this morning
It was 7:15
    Usually
        a few minutes
           earlier
But it felt good
    My dreams
        disturbed
           by the need
I'll let you know
    if anything
        else important
           pops
               up

Beyond the Road

Take a walk
    on the mild side
Skating
    on easy street
Wondering
    when the
        hot chocolate
Will kick
    in

JT Curran

2 days ago
    my Dad
        was born
88 years ago
    birthdays
        come and
            go
Even when you're
        dead
Just ask
    George Washington

Beyond the Road

Hell
    had no meaning
        for Pagans
So
    we introduced
        the concept
    Killed them
        if they didn't buy
            into it
And
    ruined a good
        thing

JT Curran

Left wing
        Right wing
How about a
        Chicken wing
Pretty hard
        to strap
                a bomb to
                      that
And
    it's quite tasty
      with BBQ
          sauce

Beyond the Road

Bones
    under the parking
           lot
Been
    missing for 500
           years
But
    somebody must have
           known
Back
    when they threw him
           down
And
    nobody gave a
           shit
Cause
    he was such an ass
           hole
Maybe
    they should leave him
           be
And
    charge extra to park
        on the spot

JT Curran

She paced
    the waiting room
Unable to sit still
    looking
        for some kind
            of diversion
"Do you like music?"
    she asked
I like the gospel station
    on cable
Putting my book down
    I took the bait
    and
        in 5 short
            minutes
She spoke 5 languages
    was 9 when Hitler
        took over her country
(Did I mention she was French)
She saw the Fuehrer once
    Almost laughed at
    the silliness
        the "Heil Hitler" salute
    and the
        youngsters
            uniformed and
            un informed
She saw Churchill
    smoking a fat cigar
    De Gaulle
    Montgomery

Beyond the Road

Somehow met a GI
    He
        born in Chicago
        raised in Ireland
        (his mother didn't like the U.S.A.)
      only
to return to his country
        to serve
I love the opera
    my father took me
        as a young girl
and she would sing
    the arias
        loud
while neighbors derided
    her
Did I drink
    she hoped not
(Sorry Babe)
Her husband
        dropped dead at 46
(must have been alcohol related)
Then....Service
    called my name
        Car's ready
Questions
    Questions
        Questions
Never to be answered
    I picked up my
        book

said goodbye
and wondered
    as I wandered to the
        service desk
She'd had a ball
    with the other woman
        who left
You know,
        the one with the
        cell phone
            that rang
mama   mama   mama
mama   mama   mama..............

Beyond the Road

Cyberspace
    filled with inane
        tweets
        emails
        and
            Facebook
                postings
Seems to be pushing
    the Holy Ghost
        out of the
            airwaves
Cause
    I haven't seen him
        for a
            long
            long
                time

JT Curran

4 Coronas
    1 phony margarita
And
    Here's to new family
Clink Clink
    and then
The guys
    talk to each
        other
The girls
    talk to each
        other
And the
    new family
        member
Sits by herself
    wondering
        why
Her husband isn't there

Beyond the Road

The band
        cranking
The old guy
        bouncing
The women
        jiggling
                giggling
and
    having so much
                fun
It puts
    a smile
        on the old
                guy
In fact
    it might even be
                a grin

JT Curran

Simply
      Put
It doesn't really
             matter
Simply
      Put
Doesn't leave much
           wiggle room
And
    To put it simply
I can't
     put up
         without
             the wiggle

Dennis Hopper
    Turns out
           he's a
                  Republican
I guess
    he was
        truly
            a method
                actor
Oh
   shatter
        my reverie
Make
   it
      a nightmare

JT Curran

Seems
      to be
a problem
       with civility
the First Amendment
      in reality
Only
    works
        when I'm
           talking

Beyond the Road

JT Curran

XII - THE RED BOOK - BETWEEN THE HOLIDAYS

Beyond the Road

The sexes
     getting closer
Equality
    moving
        more and
            more
to the middle
        ground that is
Before
   you know it
      the remote
        is no longer
  a
     masculine
        object
Whatta
    we
       watchin'
          Babe

JT Curran

Another
    Psycho
Dons
    his armor
        loads
            his clips
And
    heads out
        to the arena
Oops
    forgot to mention
        kills his father
            &
                brother
He's ready
    Bro
        Guess
            a background
                check
            won't be
                    needed
                        for this
                            Dude
Like a video
        game
            He
                shoots
                    every
                    one
                      he
                        sees

Beyond the Road

Dark
    Dreary
        Rain
Cold
    Chilly
        Pain
Mostly
    Depressing
        Lonely
            Feelings
Like
    some evil
        force
            is lurking
                behind
                    the clouds
Waiting
    for the
        right
            moment
                to strike

JT Curran

    ?
Quiet
    so quiet
You can
    hear the molecules
        ever so
            gentle
                bumping into
                    one
                        another
It's
    tranquility
You can
    sense the moment
        right here
            right
                now
Quiet
    so heavy
You can
    feel redeemed
        smile
            right here
                right
                    now
And
    then some
        happy go lucky
            dick head

Beyond the Road

Comes
    whipping by
        on a four wheeler
The
    moment
        passes

JT Curran

```
Loon
     at night
Echoing
     across
          the lake
Wonder
     what he's
          saying
               asking
                    pleading
Crying
     in the night
The
   Loon
```

Beyond the Road

Independence
        Day
    Of party
        Day
   Of debauchery
        Day
To let loose
    with the burgers
        and dogs
Beer galore
    Food
        and
            More food
Cherry bombs
      and bottle rockets
Waiting
    for the big show
        the big glow
Waiting
    for the alcohol
        to kick in
Great
    for the kids
Teaches them
    the cost of freedom
Shit
   hot dogs are
      4 bucks for
        an 8 pack now
   forget
      the rolls

JT Curran

The sun
    turned pink
    smeared
        across the sky
Like a Monet
    or
        Manet
One of those
    impressionists
        You know
What I'm talking about
As
  the night
      approached
Fading
    to gray
Fading
    away
      Going
        Going
          Gone

Beyond the Road

I wish
   Batman
      was around
When I
   walked into
      that redneck
         wayside bar
in Arkansas
When
   all those assholes
   stared hard
   and drooled
At the thought
      of ripping me apart
Oh yeah
   With Batman
      beside me
I could've yelled
   "What the fuck
      are you looking at
         Dick heads!"
Let the chips
      fall

August 6 or 7

She
   caught my
          eye
You
   know
      a simple
         glance
But
   there
      was more
         to it
The glance
    had
       a sensual
          thing
Like
  a
     hidden agenda
Item
   number
       five
Meet me
     in the parking
          lot

Beyond the Road

Man
    you gotta slow
            down
    Relax
You
    don't need another
            thing
Cause they
        never stop
        the need
        the thing
        the needs
        the things
Before you
        know it
You're
    6 feet
        below the
            surface
Then
    you'll relax

JT Curran

9-11 eve
   On the edge
        the brink
            the next step
Being
   Ka boom
Haven't had a good
            war
    for at least
      20
         minutes
Where's
    Sun Tzu
      when
        you need
           him

Beyond the Road

The shadows
    are moving
        sneaking
            through the trees
Standing
    guard
        disappearing
            when I approach
Can't tell
    if they're
        after me
Or maybe
    warning
        impending
Doom
    on the way
Don't
    think
        my heart
            can take
                it
                    either way

JT Curran

The Hippies
    are aging
Replacing
    Bells
       with cargo
          shorts
            and crocs
Others
     with canes
        and wheelchairs
Moving
    through
        the crowd
Trying
   to remember
When
   the days
      meant
         something
When
   the world
      was
        ripe for change
Wondering
    what could
       have
         been

Beyond the Road

Honking
    in the morn
   V-formed
     skimming
           the trees
Determination
    Get in line
         gang
   We got
      a ways
         to go

JT Curran

I was
    wishing
        to talk to you
        in a
            big way
Missing
    the moments
        when somehow
        I felt
            better
Afterwards
    I guess
        it was just
        hearing
            your voice
Knowing
    you were
        still around
        if I
            needed
Something
    you were
        still around
Knowing

Beyond the Road

It
  occurred to me
that
  I don't give a shit
What
   you think
But
   It still pisses
             me off
When
     you say the
         things
            you do
Even
    assholes
        have a right
To
    express their
      fucked up
         ideas
But
    yours take
       the prize

JT Curran

November
    peeking around
        the corner
Cold air
    seeping
        into the bones
And
    the new pope
    warms
        the air
Making
    November
        seem
            further away
And
    he did it
        so
            effortlessly
Miracles
        already

Beyond the Road

Just when
    I think
        the connection
            is working
You email
    me
        some stupid
            right wing
                redneck
                    joke
Written
    by
        some dim-witted
            asshole
                who thinks
                    he's
A genius
    and
        you think
            I might
                get a kick
                    out of
                        it
Time passes
    what
        happened
            to you
                ?

JT Curran

The remote
    passes
        he knows
That she'll
    watch shit
        he doesn't care for
But she
    tries to find
        a happy
            medium
        to watch
            something
        that they'll
            both
                like
Or at least
    something
        that won't
            make her
                sick
In the end
    she
        probably
            should have
                left
The remote
        remote
            and said
Let's listen
    to some
        music

Beyond the Road

Here son
    take my
        gun to school
Show and tell
    Show your friends
    Tell them it's
            loaded
    Watch the
        fun
When things
        calm down
    Tell them
        again
Why
    Daddy
        needs
        a
Concealed
    Weapon
        Permit

JT Curran

Muffled applause
    gloved rooters
        trying to ignore
            the cold
Sounds like
    flapping
        wings
    thousands
        of birds
            trying
To raise
    the team
        up a level
            but
They can't
    seem to get
    off
        the ground
Heading south
    is only
        a metaphor

Beyond the Road

As
   the world
         crumbles
To add
     insult
         to injury
We face
    a Velveeta
         shortage
What
    the fuck
        is the
            world
Coming to

JT Curran

Diminished
        Libido
Yeah
    My dick
        is getting smaller
            every day
Eventually
    I'll be
        able to
            fuck myself
            from
          the inside
                out

Beyond the Road

Anticipation
      Never
           Quite
Lives up
     to expectations
Anticipation
      Sometimes
          Much
Better
    than the
           experience
Experience
      Anticipation
           And
You'll
    always be
        ahead
           of
        the game
Pre
   Mature
        Articulation

JT Curran

The stars
        disappear
Clouds
     the atmosphere
With a
     hazy fear
        of the
            impending
                storm
Building
    Bubbling
        Ready to burst
            a thirst
                to cover
            The landscape
                with inches
                    of snow white
                        flakes
Like fingerprints
        not one
            the same

Perplexing
    Tracks in the snow
Like
    real angel
        wings
    perfect feathers
        placed
          like a faint
            photograph
Wondered
  what
    was going on
Put
  a little mystery
        in the day
Forensics
    in the
      woods

JT Curran

Eating
    with chop sticks
    Chinese food
Love
    the feel
        and realize
            why
Most of the Chinese people
                no obesity
Utensils
    with limited
        bites
Not like
    Americans
We
  use
      shovels

Beyond the Road

Been
    thinking 'bout
          my Dad
Wondering
    where he's been
        the
last 5 years
Wondering
    what jewels
        of wisdom
he forgot
to impart
Wondering
    why I sound
        more and more
    like him
    every day
Been
    thinking 'bout
          my Dad
Wondering

JT Curran

The guys
    standing
        round the campfire
Passing
    a joint
    making small
        talk
Dissing
    the left
        for no apparent
            reason
The gals
    gathered
    round the table
Wine
    in hand
    making small talk
Fracking
    friends
        for no apparent
            reason

Beyond the Road

We
   were young once
I've
   got the photos
         to prove it
Virile
   strong
       good looking
Bopping
     around
        like we owned the world
I've
   got the photos
         to prove it
Laughing
   playing
      having a great time
I've
   got those photos
   If only
        I could remember
          where
             I put them

JT Curran

Beyond the Road

JT Curran

XIII -RECENT WORK

Beyond the Road

Summer Solstice
    Father's Day
Wonder
      is it cyclic or
      just an anomaly
Doesn't matter
Raining like a bastard
Cold as oxymoronic hell
I wait
    for praise
A good father's
      reward
"I love you Dad"
I can't
    pass it upward
The gates
    are closed
And seems like
    no one's listening
Love you Dad
    Miss you a lot

JT Curran

Clare
    was there
    I swear
She didn't care
       air
Was free
    and
        she was still
            breathing

Jack

New stone
    Fresh out of the box
The guy in control
    Finally sprung for it
Makes it a bit easier
    To find
    Odd
How he got control
    Over all the words
And he never
    Wrote a single
        syllable
Right place
    Right time
        Right sister
Feel the money
    rolling in

JT Curran

Burt
    the Bee man
Ever
       see one
No more -
     Took the journey
Obit said
     he died at home
Surrounded
     by family and friends
Didn't know
     he had any
Anyway
    Been here
        Done it
           Gone
Wonder if the queen
    shed a tear

Beyond the Road

   Hey kid
      What kind of bullshit
       You be pulling
      Playing the bad guy
         Talking that trash
           like a flash
     You'll disappear
      And very few
         will remember
    The person
       You coulda been
Wake up
    Sucka

All
    of a sudden
The past
    seems important
    remembering
          things
That
    fewer
        &
          fewer
              know
People
      Places
          Things
          That happened
And
    no one
        to share
            The thoughts
            Moments
                That were

Beyond the Road

Put the boy
     in the dryer
That'll teach
     the little fucker
There are
        boundaries
            rules
You can't cross
Number One
    Do what I say
    When I say
        And don't give
           me any shit
Got it!
Or
  is it time
        to dry the clothes

JT Curran

Mill towns
    closing down
Everybody
    wipes their ass
        with Chinese paper
Communication
    electric airwaves
    battery powered
            images
Nobody
    gives a shit
    about the workforce
Only
    those involved
Daily lives
    filled with fear
          and anger
Meanwhile
    the world talks
      with thumbs
        and eyes

Beyond the Road

All Saints
    All Souls
Can't seem to remember
    which is which
        and
    which is when
Anyway
    November first
    Ash trees empty
    Maples clinging
    No wind
    Gray sky
    One by one
        they flutter
            to the ground

JT Curran

Sometimes
    I feel like
        everything's perfect
For a moment
        nothing could be
            any better
Sometimes
    I feel like
        I might burst
For the moment
        with love
            and laughter
Sometimes
    I feel like
        content
Know what I mean?
But
    this ain't
        one of those times
Close
    but the cigar
        is out of sight

Beyond the Road

What
    kind of hopelessness
Must
    you feel
        to strap a vest
        loaded to the max
        explosives
To kill
    unsuspecting fellow
        human beings
No feeling of remorse
    just a vague
        promise of a few
        thousand virgin
            blow jobs
Yeah man
    you're gonna get
        blown
            from here
                to there
And you're gonna miss
    the orgasm

JT Curran

We'd
    hop in that old VW
    rattle down the road
        to the old schoolhouse
  a future palace
  a vision
  a place to get away
  do some destructive
        renovation
    Open it up
        explore the 2X4's
        real 2X4's
            no insulation
    Possibilities endless
        just need some cash
We'd
    tear it apart
    cover ourselves with dust
And just maybe
    end with a cold
        thirst-quenching beer
Save the joint
    for the ride
        home

Beyond the Road

Gathered
    in the town hall
    rough looking
        crowd
Hinting at
    cigarettes
    beer
        and Harleys
Farewell tribute
    thought there might be
        a microphone
        an emcee
    a chance to share
Not a group to let their
        guard down
Come on
    let's shed a few tears
        here
Guaranteed to make
    you feel better
And just maybe
    that's what he
        might have wanted

Legacy
       age old problem
What did I do
What was accomplished
       that someone
       might remember
or maybe
       just maybe
            something important
like
   a footnote
       in history books
or
   a cult
   a movement
   a difference
or
   at the least
      a mention
         at the pub
Raise your glass
   and put it on my tab

Roller skating
    Sometime in the mid 50's
    Mrs. Roy
    Helen
Part of the young
      war hero families
Took us all roller skating
    First time
Youngsters
    Nothing
        could hurt us
Fall after fall
    we started to get it
Helen
    our hero
Watching over us
    while her husband
    was fucking whoever
        he could
Teaching us
    Taking care
      Took a tumble
      Broke both collar bones
Sorry Mr. Roy
    You're gonna have to
      jerk off
        for a few weeks

JT Curran

Breezy
        Palm trees
Golf balls
      going
              left and right
Brown-skinned
        Northerners
Tapping
       and gabbing
Working
       the rounds
Waiting
      for happy hour

Need
      a new camp sign
Old one's had it
Don't want to sound
              cheap
But
      what's the cheapest
                you got
Last 5 to 7 years
That's plenty
          of time
Won't be around
          for the end
Shit man
      kind of cutting
          your life short
Guess
      you don't have
         much to look
              forward to
Maybe
      a new camp sign
         will do it

Birthday eve
    2016
Watching
    the Lightning and
        Penguins
Never seen too many
    aggressive Penguins
Lightning is always
        volatile
Smash crash bang
Looks like the Penguins
    don't stand a chance
        gonna be ashes
But then again
It's birthday eve
And
    those Penguins
    are
        oh so cute

Beyond the Road

I've been thinking
           about you a lot
                    lately
Makes me think of me
          and wonder
          am I the asshole
                  or you
I mean
        deep down
I know it's you
And so do you
Yet
        I still blame myself
        Thinking
              I did everything
                          wrong
      Knowing
           I should have been
                      better
But in the end
        You're still an asshole
Doesn't
        make me feel
                any better

JT Curran

```
Trying
        to think of something
                        Poignant
Great word
        Great idea
                Turn your head
Thinking
        Thoughts of movement
                Twirling
                        round and round
Listen
        I am getting ready
            to say
                    something
                Very
                        Poignant
```

Beyond the Road

That 54 Cadillac
    or was it a Buick
Anyway
    Convertible
    Top down
    Back seat
    Filled with
    Folded newspapers
Each day
    A race
    To finish
    Cutting corners
    Tossing to
        the wind
    Driveways
    Blurred as you
        picked up speed
        60 by the turn around
Hey
    Let's do the other side

JT Curran

The late night train
    coming up from
           Clarksburg
           Tennessee
Late was the night train
Getting quieter
Getting spookier
    Like a misty fog in a London thriller
Waiting
    for a girl from
        Alabama
A scene
    from a Faulkner novel
Getting ready
For a night
    of disappointment
For both
    of us

Beyond the Road

The silence
   as Fall turns
       the next page
Pure
   Moments of time
   Lost in memory
       no images
       just feelings
The silence
   as Fall turns
       the next page
Ominous
   Threads of time
   Lost memories
       no images
       just feelings
Silence
    I feel honored
    to share it
       with the Universe

JT Curran

Concussion
        Protocol
Does your brain
              feel like jello
Are your eyes
              like pinballs
Can you see
              this waiver
Sign it
        Here's a pen

Beyond the Road

Wish
    I'd a known
It
   was going so fast
Might
   have paid more attention
To
   all the things
           put off
Maybe
     slowed things
             down a bit
Relaxed
     a bit more
Loved
     a lot more
Learned
     a great more
Lived
     a beat more
Like the drummer
         says
Thumpity thump thump
            Splang

JT Curran

Special thanks to:

Twinkle Manning for her expertise and knowledge of the publishing world;

Jason Curran for his insight and dedication to the project;

Aaron Curran for his artistic eye and enthusiasm;

Kate Peters for her photographic ability and encouragement;

Bob Loughrey for the painting on the cover and 60 years of friendship.

JT Curran

Publisher's Note

Matrika Press is an independent publishing house dedicated to publishing inspiring and thought-provoking works. We are honored to publish this collection of poems by JT Curran.

JT's poetry reflects a personal experience of his material and illustrates poetic observations readers may find both familiar and surprising. In his words we are given spontaneous prose, keen regard of things seen and unseen, and encapsulations of the essence of the human experience, even the parts we often attempt to keep hidden.
JT does all this and more, sometimes in a single poem.

Ironic one moment, deeply compassionate the next, JT's work reflects a life lived on one's own terms. It is with gratitude we present to you, "Beyond the Road."

For more information, visit:

www.MatrikaPress.com

About the Author

J.T. Curran moved to central Maine in the early 1970s, drawn in part by the homesteading movement which resonated with many who sought a rural lifestyle and greater connection to the land. He built a log cabin on his twenty-two acres of wooded paradise and helped raise three children with his partner of forty-seven years. He has worked as a woodsman and a carpenter, has cultivated his own fruits and vegetables, and has volunteered with many civic and arts organizations. He holds an M.A in Counseling and has provided counseling service to many individuals and groups. He has taught courses in psychology at the University of Maine and Eastern Maine Community College, and has had a twenty-five year career in education as a guidance counselor.

In addition to literary pursuits, J.T. is an active musician who has performed since his days in high school, where he sang doo-wop with fellow crooners in the Philadelphia based quartet, the Violators. He maintains an active performance schedule, singing and playing his guitar in venues throughout central Maine.

www.MatrikaPress.com/jt-curran

AVAILABLE NOW FROM MATRIKA PRESS

www.MatrikaPress.com

COMING SOON FROM MATRIKA PRESS

MORE MATRIKA PRESS TITLES

a Pocketful of Transcendentalism by Polly Peterson

Women of Spirit, Sacred Paths of Wisdom Keepers Anthology

Where the Sky has No Stars by Wesley Burton

Equinox by Desiray Howes

Therese's Dream by Dr. David Austin

Intimate Insights to Revolutionizing Intimacy by Tziporah Kingsbury

Joyous Everyday Living by Beth Amine

Making a Monster by Sue Humphries

www.MatrikaPress.com

www.MatrikaPress.com
ISBN:978-1-946088-01-7

www.ingramcontent.com/pod-product-compliance
Lightning Source LLC
Chambersburg PA
CBHW021429080526
44588CB00009B/466